I Know Someone with Epilepsy

Vic Parker

www.raintreepublishers.co.uk
Visit our website to find out
more information about
Raintree books.

To order:
☎ Phone 0845 6044371
🖷 Fax +44 (0) 1865 312263
🖳 Email myorders@raintreepublishers.co.uk

Customers from outside the UK please telephone +44 1865 312262

Raintree is an imprint of Capstone Global Library
Limited, a company incorporated in England and
Wales having its registered office at 7 Pilgrim Street,
London, EC4V 6LB – Registered company number:
6695582

Text © Capstone Global Library Limited 2011
First published in hardback in 2011
First published in paperback in 2012
The moral rights of the proprietor have been asserted.

Edited by Rebecca Rissman, Dan Nunn,
   and Catherine Veitch
Designed by Steve Mead and Joanna Hinton Malivoire
Picture research by Tracy Cummins
Originated by Capstone Global Library
Printed and bound in China by Leo Paper Products Ltd

ISBN 978 1 406 22080 3 (hardback)
15 14 13 12 11
10 9 8 7 6 5 4 3 2 1

ISBN 978 1 406 22354 5 (paperback)
16 15 14 13 12 11
10 9 8 7 6 5 4 3 2 1

British Library Cataloguing in Publication Data
Parker, Victoria.
I know someone with epilepsy. –
(Understanding health issues)
616.8'53-dc22
A full catalogue record for this book is available from
the British Library.

Acknowledgements
We would like to thank the following for permission
to reproduce photographs: AP Photo p. 23 (Mike
Lawrence/The Gleaner); Corbis pp. 10 (© Ariel
Skelley/Blend Images), 12 (© Bloomimage), 13 (©
Tim Pannell), 14 (© Randy Faris), 27 (© Corbis); Getty
Images pp. 6 (artpartner-images), 8 (Altrendo Images),
17 (Sean Justice), 19 (Robert E Daemmrich), 22 (LM
Productions), 24 (Andrew H. Walker), 25 (Mick Hutson/
Redferns); istockphoto pp. 4 (© Steve Cole), 5 (©
Pamela Moore), 11 (© Mark Kostich), 15 (© Francisco
Romero), 18 (© Bonnie Jacobs); Photo Researchers,
Inc. p. 16 (Annabella Bluesky); Shutterstock pp. 20 (©
Mandy Godbehear), 21 (© Andreas Gradin).

Cover photograph of a father and two children in the
snow reproduced with permission of Getty Images
(Caroline Woodham).

We would like to thank Ashley Wolinski and Matthew
Siegel for their invaluable help in the preparation of
this book.

Every effort has been made to contact copyright
holders of any material reproduced in this book. Any
omissions will be rectified in subsequent printings if
notice is given to the publisher.

Contents

Some words are printed in bold, **like this**. You can find out what they mean in the glossary.

Do you know someone with epilepsy?

You may have a friend with epilepsy. Epilepsy is an illness that causes **seizures**. A seizure is something that happens in someone's **brain**. It can affect their senses, behaviour, feelings, or thoughts for a while.

If you have a friend who has epilepsy, you can still play whatever you want with them.

Someone with epilepsy may wear a bracelet or necklace to let others know.

Often, you cannot tell that somebody has epilepsy. Unless a person is actually having a seizure, there is normally nothing unusual to see.

What is a seizure?

Just as a computer uses electricity to work, so do our **brains**. Our brains send electrical messages all around our bodies. These control everything we think, do, and say.

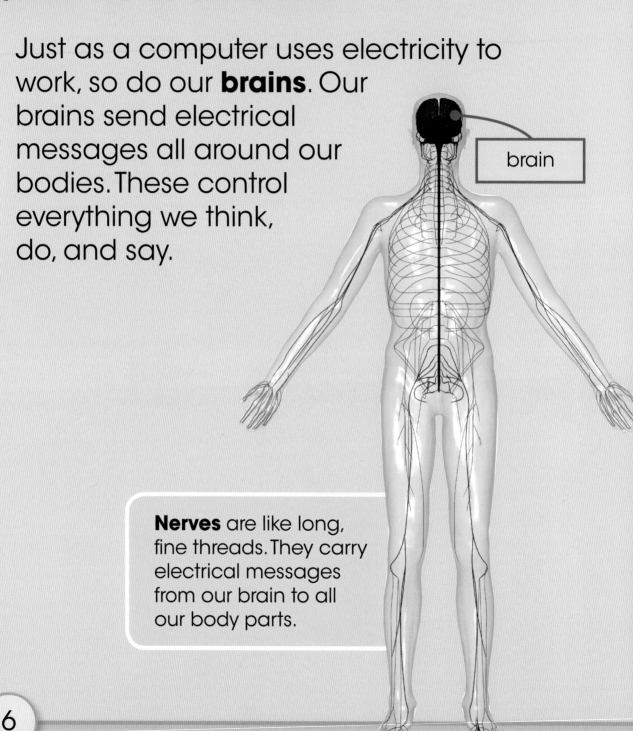

brain

Nerves are like long, fine threads. They carry electrical messages from our brain to all our body parts.

When a **seizure** happens, there is too much electricity in a person's brain. This can have all sorts of effects on their body, depending on the part of their brain it happens in.

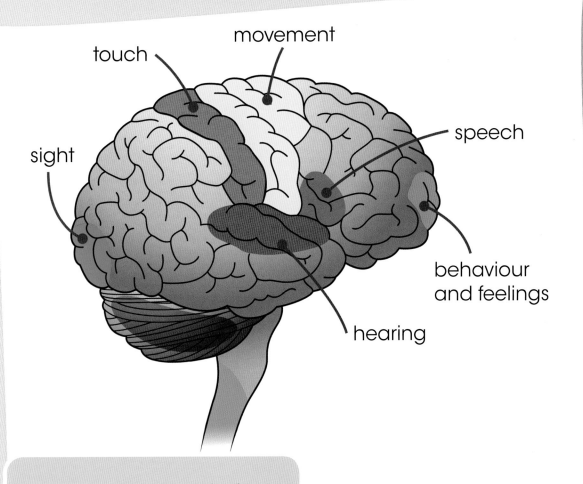

touch

movement

sight

speech

behaviour and feelings

hearing

This picture shows just a few of the things different parts of our brain control.

How do seizures affect people?

There are many different types of **seizure**. Some types of seizure make people confused. Some types make people move or make noises. Some types make people still or silent.

Some seizures can last only a few seconds, others can last for two minutes or more.

Some people have seizures in which they fall down and their body shakes. If this happens, you can help by:

- sending someone to tell an adult and call an ambulance
- laying the person down on his or her back or side
- putting something soft under the person's head
- loosening any tight clothing
- moving everything away from the person, so he or she can't hit things and get hurt.

The causes of seizures

There are many reasons why a person might have a **seizure**. They may have injured their head in an accident. Or they could have an illness that can affect the **brain**, like cancer.

A baby or toddler who is unwell can have a seizure if they have a very high temperature.

Doctors can do a special test to find out if a person has epilepsy.

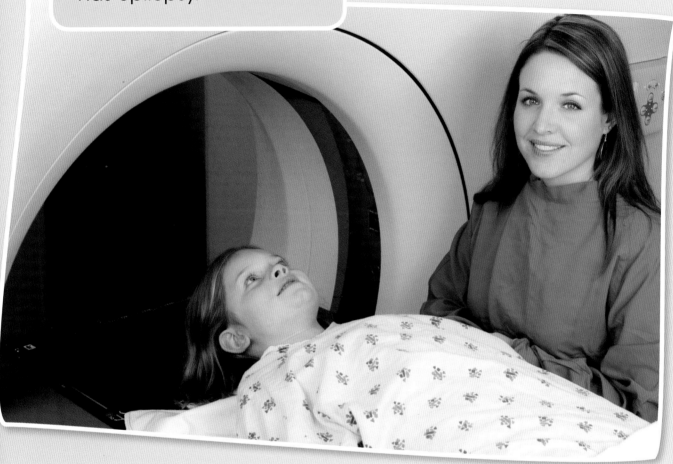

However, some people have seizures for no reason and which happen often. This illness is called epilepsy.

Who gets epilepsy?

You may be slightly more likely to develop epilepsy if someone else in your family has it.

Epilepsy can happen to any person at any age. It doesn't matter what race they are or where they live. However, it most often begins in young children or older adults.

Doctors do not know why certain people get epilepsy, but they do know that people don't always have it for their whole life. Young children who have epilepsy often grow out of it.

Many scientists are working hard to find out what causes epilepsy and how to prevent it.

Treatments for epilepsy

Some people with epilepsy can have an **operation** on their **brain** to stop the **seizures**. This cure only works for a few people. Most can only try to stop seizures from happening by taking medicine.

Some people with epilepsy need more medicine than others.

Avoiding **starchy foods** such as bread, and eating **fatty foods** can help some people with epilepsy.

For some people the medicine works, but it can make them grumpy or unable to concentrate or keep still. A few find it does not work at all. Following a special diet can help instead.

Living with epilepsy

Some people know when they are going to have a **seizure**. They may see, smell, or taste funny things, or they may get butterflies in their tummy.

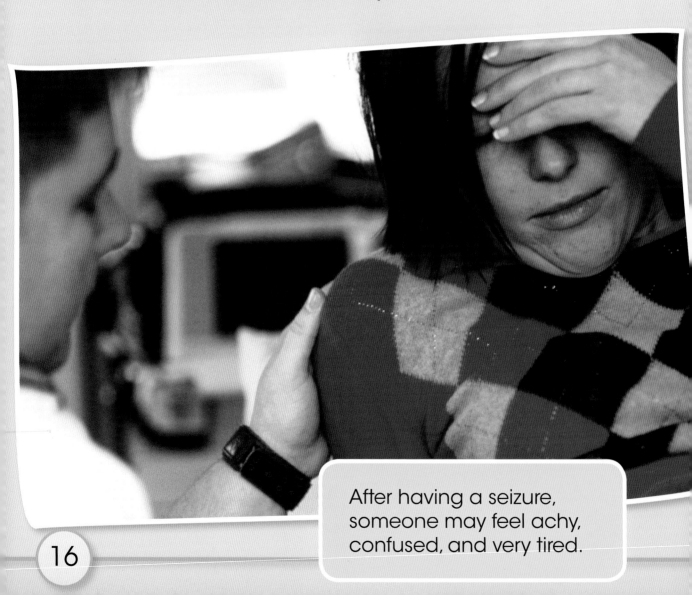

After having a seizure, someone may feel achy, confused, and very tired.

People who have their epilepsy under control are able to do activities like climbing and swimming.

People with epilepsy can do most things other people can. However, some people choose not to do activities which could be dangerous if they suddenly had a seizure.

At school

Most children with epilepsy are able to go to school with all their friends. However, many find having **seizures** embarrassing. It helps if everyone in the class knows what is happening.

A child with epilepsy may have school friends with other medical **conditions**, such as **allergies** or asthma.

Children who often have seizures where they go still for a short time may miss parts of their lessons. Teachers, parents, and friends should watch out for this, and then help them to catch up.

Working together can help a child with epilepsy do well at school and be happy.

At play

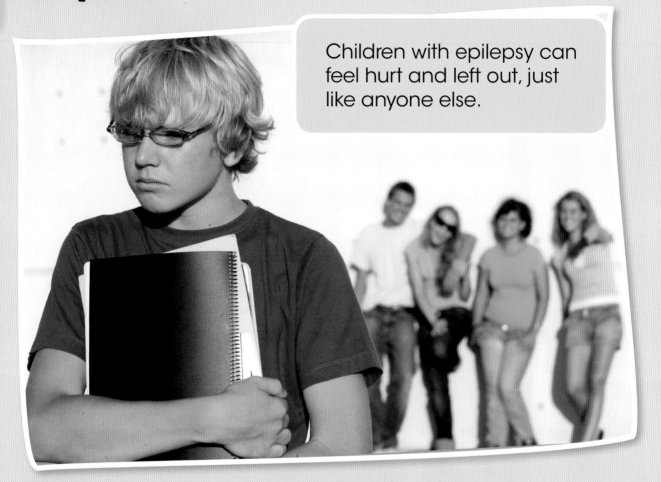

Children with epilepsy can feel hurt and left out, just like anyone else.

Most children with epilepsy love playtime and sport, just like other children. There is no reason for them not to join in with fun activities.

It is important for all children, including children who have epilepsy, to have good friends and spend time playing together. Friends can make them feel less anxious about their **seizures**. Friends can help them feel more confident.

Children with epilepsy can be very good at sport.

Living independently

Adults with epilepsy can make choices which help them live on their own. For instance, carpet is better than hard flooring. Then if they fall when they have a **seizure**, they are less likely to get hurt.

Taking a shower is better than a bath, as someone having a seizure could slip under bath water.

Some people with epilepsy use dogs or wear helmets to help protect them.

Some adults with epilepsy have a dog that is trained to warn them that they are going to have a seizure. They can then get to a safe place and get help.

Famous people

Danny Glover had epilepsy from ages 15 to 35. This didn't stop him becoming a top Hollywood actor who has starred in films including *Top Gun*, *Antz*, *The Shaggy Dog*, and the *Lethal Weapon* films.

Danny Glover used to hear a strange noise as a warning that he was going to have a seizure.

Comedian Rik Mayall takes medicines to help stop him getting seizures.

Rik Mayall is a British comedy actor who stars in many top TV shows. He has had **seizures** since he injured his head in a serious quad bike accident.

Being a good friend

There are many ways you can be a good friend to someone with epilepsy, such as:

- include your friend in everything you do with your other friends
- if you go swimming, stick by your friend at all times in case they have a **seizure**
- if your friend has a seizure, stay calm.

We all have different bodies and different personalities.

Living with epilepsy can be difficult at times. But there are many other ways in which we are all different. A good friend likes us just as we are.

Epilepsy – facts and fiction

Facts

- Around 50 million people in the world suffer from epilepsy.

- Someone with epilepsy may be more likely to have a seizure if they are unwell, stressed, tired, or hungry.

Fiction

(?) People with epilepsy aren't as intelligent as other people.

WRONG! People with epilepsy can be as intelligent as anyone else.

(?) People with epilepsy can't play video games.

WRONG! Anyone can be **sensitive** to flickering lights. But only a tiny number of people with epilepsy are affected by flickering lights. So most people with epilepsy can play video games.

Glossary

allergies bad reaction in the body to something that a person touches, breathes, eats, or drinks

brain body part inside your skull that controls all other parts of your body and that helps you to think

condition something that affects the way some parts of the body work

fatty foods foods such as butter, mackerel fish, milk, and cheese

nerves long, thin threads that carry information between body parts and the brain

operation type of medical treatment carried out in a hospital by a doctor called a surgeon

seizure disturbance in someone's brain that can affect their senses, behaviour, feelings, or thoughts for a while

sensitive quickly and easily affected by something

starchy foods foods such as bread, pasta, and potatoes

Find out more

Books to read

Living with Epilepsy
Patsy Westcott (Wayland, 2006)

Seizure-Alert Dogs (Dog Heroes)
Margaret Fetty (Bearport Publishing, 2009)

What Does It Mean to Have Epilepsy?
Louise Spilsbury (Heinemann Library, 2003)

Websites

**http://kidshealth.org/kid/health_problems/
brain/epilepsy.html**
Find out more about epilepsy.

**http://kidshealth.org/kid/word/s/word_
seizure.html**
This website explains about seizures.

http://www.youthepilepsy.com/
This website is written by a sufferer of epilepsy.

Index